ANGELICUS

"What a gift *Angelicus* is to us. . . . In this, Martin's most exploratory and creative volume of poems yet, the angels speak volumes: . . . as avengers and jokesters 'play[ing] on the edge of anarchy' as well as compassionate witnesses to human frailty 'scheming to undermine grief.' Like his clever angels, Martin's lines 'spiral' as they make 'criss-cross flights' across the pages, providing deft, inevitable rhymes and inventive turns of phrase alike. And most of all, these earnest angels know their place as 'mere messengers' . . . reminding us that '[n]o angel or demon / can separate [us] from the love of the Lord.'"

—JULIE L. MOORE, author of *Full Worm Moon*.

"This is not a book about angels; it is a book *of* angels, one that promises to bend your imagination open to a wider frame of angelic—and human— experience than you'd previously dared to know. . . . Through the eyes of Martin's angels, quirky and unpredictable as these messengers are wont to be, we come to glimpse familiar things in the dappled light of paradox. . . . In poem after poem we find ourselves called to upend a merely critical reason and enter, through the poet's wit, a realm of vision where we begin to recognize how it is that '[s]o often you look at something / without really seeing it.' This is a book that calls us to look again, expecting to see in ways that widen our apprehension of the truth . . . and might well remake us for the better."

—MARK S. BURROWS, author of *The Chance of Home*

"Martin has found his poetic voice, voicing the angels. These are celestial beings who know how to play with words, who love to alliterate, rap internal rhymes, and turn deft and memorable phrases. And they do it all with passion and wit, while never for a moment losing sight of the profound seriousness of their mission from God to us children of clay, and working tirelessly behind the scenes and before our unseeing eyes, keeping their keen yet sympathetic sights on all that makes us human and flawed, noble and delusional, and somehow still mightily loved by our Creator . . . A heavenly host of praises for these poems, and this book."

—JOHN TERPSTRA, author of *Mischief*

"In alternating moves—flights of fancy and sudden gravity—Martin offers a fine contemporary take regarding our surround of messengers."

—SCOTT CAIRNS, author of *Slow Pilgrim: The Collected Poems*

Angelicus

POEMS

D.S. MARTIN

CASCADE *Books* • Eugene, Oregon

ANGELICUS
Poems

Poiema Poetry Series

Cascade Books
An Imprint of Wipf and Stock Publishers
199 W. 8th Ave., Suite 3
Eugene, OR 97401

www.wipfandstock.com

PAPERBACK ISBN: 978-1-6667-0381-8
HARDCOVER ISBN: 978-1-6667-0382-5
EBOOK ISBN: 978-1-6667-0383-2

Cataloguing-in-Publication data:

Names: Martin, D.S., author.

Title: Angelicus : poems / D.S. Martin.

Description: Eugene, OR: Cascade Books, 2021. | Poiema Poetry Series. | Includes bibliographical references and index.

Identifiers: ISBN 978-1-6667-0381-8 (paperback). | ISBN 978-1-6667-0382-5 (hardcover). | ISBN 978-1-6667-0383-2 (ebook).

Subjects: LCSH: Poetry. | Christian poetry. | Canadian poetry--21st century.

Classification: PR9199.3 M3857 A7 2021 (print). | PR9199.3 (ebook).

In memory of
Rod Jellema
(1927–2018)

Did Jacob, his father, understand
the dream of the ladder? Or did his enduring
its mystery make him richer?
—LI-YOUNG LEE

Are not all angels ministering spirits sent to serve
those who will inherit salvation?
—HEBREWS 1:14

Table of Contents

Preface | xiii
Of Angels Speaking | 1

-one-

An Angel's View of Automobiles | 5
An Angel Marvels at Human Language | 6
Not the Winged Messengers | 7
An Angel Laughs about Laundry | 8
An Angel of Mercy Schemes to Undermine Grief | 9
Curiously More | 10
Staircase | 11
Fear Not | 12
Learning to Fly | 13

-two-

An Angel Critiques Caravaggio's *Saint Matthew & the Angel* | 17
Reflection for Elizabeth Barrett Browning | 18
Goodnight Sweet Prince | 19
Michael the Defender | 20
Putto Putto Putti | 21
Angel of Revolution | 22
Angel of Comfort   Angel of Peace | 23
The Angel of Death at the Grand Ole Opry | 24
What an Angel Admires | 25

-three-

An Angel Questions Our Answers | 29
Jacob Wrestles | 30
The Angels Watch You Fall | 31
Angel Dream | 32
An Angel Speaks of Eden's Fruit | 33
East of Eden | 34
An Angel Questions Our Questions | 35
This Same Jesus | 36
Angelic Manifestations | 37

-four-

The Angels' Vineyard Song | 41
Rain | 42
Birds of the Air | 43
Frozen Lake | 44
Polar Bear | 45
Your Cat Watching | 46
Coram Deo | 47
An Angel from Signorelli's *Resurrection of the Body* | 48
An Angel from Cimabue's *The Crucifixion* | 49

-five-

Sitting on a Stone | 53
Intervening Angel | 54
Liberating Angel | 55
Avenging Angel | 56
Ministering Angel | 57
A Guardian Angel in the Dominican Republic | 58
A Gathering Angel Tries to Stay Alert | 59
In the Early Morning | 60
An Angel Watches *It's a Wonderful Life* | 61

-six-

The Angel of the Church in Toronto Writes | 65
The Burning Heart | 66

TABLE OF CONTENTS

An Angel on Married Love | 67

Cherubim | 68

Seraphim | 69

An Angel Addresses a Churchgoer | 70

An Angel's Asked about William Blake | 71

An Angel Denies a Flat Earth | 72

An Angel Speaks of Living Things | 73

-seven-

The Tenth Plague | 77

Murder Mystery | 79

Teen Angel | 80

An Angel Explains Prayer | 81

Preannunciation | 82

Sky Choir | 83

Swing Low Sweet Grocery Cart | 84

Response to Rilke | 85

Surreal Orchid | 86

Acknowledgements | 87

Preface

SCRIPTURE PRESENTS ANGELS AS they appear in stories, without making much effort to explain. The line between an angel who comes to serve God and an angel who actually is God is confoundingly crisscrossed in many of these accounts. I have made some effort to make crooked lines straight, but have not always made the rough places plain. Forgive me whenever my angels erroneously cross this important, but hard to perceive, line.

So many unexamined snippets concerning angels have trickled into our brains from every conceivable angle. I have had fun mocking many of these; our susceptibility to them, though comes from the Bible's information-vacuum on the subject. Whenever Biblical angels appear in human guise—for example—they seem to be male, yet I would hesitate to suggest that a shimmering being of beauty and goodness could not conversely appear in a more feminine form.

Some of the poets who have whispered their way into these pages include Dante Alighieri, W.H. Auden, William Blake, Elizabeth Barrett Browning, Emily Dickinson, John Donne, Lawrence Ferlinghetti, Seamus Heaney, John Milton, Rainer Maria Rilke, William Shakespeare, and Richard Wilbur. Perhaps a dozen ancient poets, whose work is found in the pages from Genesis to Revelation, have also been faithfully plagiarized.

Soli Deo Gloria,
DSM

OF ANGELS SPEAKING

When we seek to speak   to such
as you   O child of clay   we confess
limited success

translating on the wing from
tongues of angels   from flaming radiance
in celestial presence   to your sheenless existence

What we say   needs traction
in your slippery language   besides fluent sound
making new use of shopworn words

in partnership   to avoid a vacuous spin
so your imagination can begin
to comprehend

We don't intend to flabbergast
but you'd ignore us   found at your back door
in jeans & human skin

We won't pretend we don't scare you   having been
coached by archangels   who've had to lift
your trembling forebears   from the ground

-one-

But who of the children of men can comprehend
what is the understanding of an angel?

—JOHN WESLEY

AN ANGEL'S VIEW OF AUTOMOBILES

      Before they talked to their cars
they talked to their horses   Not just the *giddy-up* & *whoa*
or the clucking tongue   but the patter of shared
days   busy streets   unending rain
      At least a carthorse could sense meaning
from the tone of a familiar voice   A mare could mimic
the melancholy of a burdensome journey
in her plodding clip clop   or mirror excitement
in an equestrian canter
      But now they speak to cold machinery
take directions from a disembodied voice
      There's nothing of the animal
human bond   no consciousness like that of Balaam's ass
to save his life from the angel's sword   nothing
about a car that can transport like Elijah' s fiery chariot
      Before they talked to their cars
some of them even talked with God

AN ANGEL MARVELS AT HUMAN LANGUAGE

Right from the start   imitating & experimenting   as infants
        once flailing fingers fail
you gurgle & burble your way toward words
You humans are all language-makers
linguistic babblers   jabberers   & risk-takers

Though you're lower than angels   we delight
in your inventions   You name every game you play
place descriptors on the tall   & the small   have a name
for every animal   & every animal-call   teased from sound   shape   &
associated word
        a glorious onomatopoetic   cock-a-doodle-doo   drawn from
every encountered hullabaloo
        & not just one for the whole world   for in every language   or
dialect   every valley identified on its own
even in every household
there's a different way to say
                something
To the south cattails sway   & further north   bulrushes wave
in the wind   while certain purists firmly insist
these terms are misapplied

When Yahweh brought the man to the table   to name each creature
we gathered to hear what each would be
Now we see   this was just a start
        how you're able to label & relabel every person   place   or part
        how you're so prone to classify   every rock & reptile   infection
& infraction   your heart must believe   you'll tame through these
names   all they signify

NOT THE WINGED MESSENGERS

All you see   is what you see
not the winged messengers who   solely
do what we're called to do
        You do not see   all that's
behind what you see   O child of clay
such as the way   bees are drawn
to the red of floral radiance   not simply
to sip nectar   or to experience
overwhelming colour   or to cross-pollinate
plants   but out of obedience
        & the daisies don't dance
in their particular whites   & yellows   & blues
simply to attract pollinators   but because
it is what they've been created to do
        The dogs live their doggy lives
as those bees return to their hives   where there
is no insurrection   The queen rules   & the drones
drone   until the cows come home
        Only your kind   O child of clay
struggles with purposelessness   the sorrow
of how you've spent your day
& what you'll do tomorrow

AN ANGEL LAUGHS ABOUT LAUNDRY

after Wilbur

If ever we wanted to hide in plain sight
it would be out in the pure light
of washday   where the homebound hope
the soap & sun will wash away each stain

Unashamed   they air their laundry   luminous & white
strung from building to balcony   at unlikely heights
where we'd fly   amid flapping frocks   & smocks
& bright billowing blouses   far above other earthly concerns

Behind suburban houses   in playful turns
& fleet flips   we'd slip our arms into shirtsleeves
or bulge bedsheets like sails for ships
if ever we wanted to hide in plain sight

Does such frivolity   strike you
as unbecoming to angels of light?
Know   then   we continually dwell in joy
& when love calls us   we respond with what's right

AN ANGEL OF MERCY SCHEMES TO UNDERMINE GRIEF

By the rivers of Babylon   women washed laundry
in their own tears   & by the Thames   those widowed
or abandoned   took in the washing of well-to-do neighbours

One woman   whose tough labours
rarely received payment enough   often scrubbed
clothes to glow   like heavenly raiment

Up to her elbows in steaming tubs
hands wrinkling red in harsh suds   her youth
flowed away in grey water

Her need was a seed   for an angel of mercy
to plant in soft soil   I found her grown daughter
able to bring her in   That's how multiplied blessings begin

CURIOUSLY MORE

You encountered three men   curiously more than men
none of whom you recognized
                    robed in white   perhaps?
who were suddenly just there   in the heat of the day
neither dismounting
                    nor about to collapse
where you wouldn't have expected anyone to be
                    three angels perhaps?
curiously more than angels   & so you shared
your water   & your shade
had bread made   & meat prepared
& when they asked after your wife   by name
who was stirring just beyond the tent flaps
                    didn't it feel the same
as when you met a certain king
                    or sound like a voice
you'd heard not long before then?

These three   disguised as angels   disguised as men

STAIRCASE

Piercing night   ascending
descending   sky to ground   our light footfalls
in fluid motion pass through air   make
no sound   No spiral   or criss-cross flights
but one uninterrupted series of stairs
ten thousand climbing angels in glowing white
ten thousand more   trodding down
down from heaven's height
from the foot of God's own throne
right down to a stone   a shaken scoundrel's
using for his pillow   Why would we wonder
    to what purpose   this display
when we know wisdom whispers   *obey*?

FEAR NOT

As light spills from my wings
      your eyes widen
& your tongue goes dry

You will not die   though you will
      change more
than at your final reckoning

My voice pours significance into
      your veins   beyond your
wildest imagining

To reassure   You have free choice
      though he who dwells
in the yet to come   knows what will be

True   you will not merely be your own
but then   you never were

LEARNING TO FLY

an angel reflects on human discovery

Before they knew how to fly   they watched birds
all that flap & flutter of feathers   A boy once tried
it himself   Icarus-like   but with less
immediate success   hauling himself to the top of a wall
only to fall   over & over again   but at least
without the plummet into the blue Mediterranean

Whenever the Maker laughed   *Watch this*
delighted by their contraptions   rattling
along the beach   for us   the angels who've never
had to learn   it was like watching them struggling to reach
God   lifted on the wind of the Spirit   but tripping
when some preacher   tied their shoelaces together

The boy wondered whether angels have feathers
though knew little of wind   & even less of weightlessness
Leonardo tried many things   knowing how to look
& guess   & learn from every fall
perhaps knowing how God loves a puzzle
the biggest   an intricate universe   made   oh so discoverable

13

-*two*-

At the last, when we die, we have the dear angels
for our escort on the way.

—MARTIN LUTHER

AN ANGEL CRITIQUES CARAVAGGIO'S *SAINT MATTHEW & THE ANGEL*

The Church of San Luigi dei Francesi, Rome

As rich as it is   his painting's
misconceived
depicting what humanity's not able
to perceive
              Overlook
the anachronisms   of
latter-day bench & table
& replacing Matthew's parchment
with a book
              Ignore
the appealing bedsheet draping the angel
who seems perplexingly suspended
from a ceiling hook   & even the twisted angle
at which the writer must look
              The inspiration that was given
isn't something he'd heard   as if recited to him
word for word   but what the altarpiece alters
what troubles me most   is would Heaven
merely send an angel
to do the work of the Holy Ghost?

REFLECTION FOR ELIZABETH BARRETT BROWNING

an angel addresses her 22nd sonnet

Despite the wrongs
      that you had to endure
   first   from illness
     from human contrariness
       then the worst   pain
    from family jealousies   turning
        them away
your two souls grew strong   with a contentment   of great gain
    like a well-stoked fire   burning
        pure & long
            in a sweet solitude
    which angels would not presume to intrude
       upon
We would not aspire *to drop some golden orb*
      of perfect song
    where it was not required
      for times are not to be prematurely absorbed
    in what's to come   since darkness shows the firelight
& your bright love   on earth
still speaks of things above

GOODNIGHT SWEET PRINCE

For you   little one   there's much unknown
about the transition   which   above your life   lifts
like a mysterious tower
As angels   we watch everyone eventually
step inside   but you see none return   or even wave
a handkerchief from the battlements
As humans   you have no power   so susceptible
to dangers you can't ignore   a major burn   a minor shift
in temperature   infection   suffocation   falling
or being fallen upon   crushed to the floor   drowning
poison   thirst & starvation   any of a thousand diseases
accident   & the bursts of war
From your timebound streets   you squint into eternity
& ask   *when* questions   I could call death   a gateway
into a hidden garden   a sleep without dreams   a flight
of angels singing you to your rest   & though it's simpler
than it seems   with your limited view   it's hard to know
which descriptor's best
For the faithful   there's nothing to fear   & since
you know who steers your craft   do you really need to ask?

MICHAEL THE DEFENDER

Spoken of as being before the world
      & after it's end   in words
           rolled up & sealed

which will not be revealed
      until then   I am sent to defend
           those in need of rest

As commander of angel armies
      what might be said of me
           to comfort the oppressed?

The iconographers have me dressed
      in a coat of mail   place my foot
           on the vanquished dragon & put

a spear in my hand   driven down
      into his roaring throat   I stand
           above his curled body in a symbolism

beyond what those in your world can see
      Why must I still say *Don't bow before me*?
           Just trust the one whose will I strive to fulfil

PUTTO PUTTO PUTTI

an angel rants about tacky images of fat winged babies

They only fly in your imaginations
baby angels   as naked as a lover's lies
decorating the architectural fringes of heathen sarcophagi
& the pottery of lost Etruscans

Why   O child of clay   would any artist   of sobriety
think such bunk   should flutter across church ceilings
to clutter congregants' pliable minds   with such angelological
                                                                junk
revealing a lack of serious piety   like some Bacchanal drunk?

We angels were created   never born
we never loiter   like a grandmother's garden gnomes
are imagined to do   Let's leave such nonsense
far from depictions of scripture   & stick to what is true

ANGEL OF REVOLUTION

I play on the edge of anarchy   risking absurdity & even
your death   a temporary problem in the grand scheme
for it's not just to defeat tyrants
                                    but to kill the tyrant within
Don't assume   that because something is labelled revolution
I had anything to do with it   Don't assume I didn't

Don't be shocked at angelic intervention in human history
It's what we do   You creatures of comfort   often need
a swift kick   to vacate easy chairs
Some have been caught by the boots of angels unawares

Like hearing   a little coal-dust-covered chimney sweep
weep   & hoping someone would bring a key
to unlock their coffins   Lord Shaftesbury found himself
surprisingly rising to his feet   to set them free

But to you   I suppose   that was long ago
& you love the idea of being a hero in a grand cause
which shows how much you love applause
exposing your own tyrannical braggart
& your deep need
                    for revolution in your heart

ANGEL OF COMFORT   ANGEL OF PEACE

Incense curls in the air
        swirls with caring intersessions
      & with your own prayers   as I swing
        my golden censer   a fragrant pendulum
      sweet smoke wafting from my hand
      before the throne

What whirling unknown   or earthly dissonance
        do you permit to rob you
      of your peace   O descendant of dust?
        Why   even beside still waters   let such
      turmoil stir heartache?

The flogged evangelists
        sang in their dank cell
      before the earthquake
escaped slaves gave thanks
        on the riverbank
      before their night crossing
& sheepherders   stumbling into Bethlehem   awe-filled
        with our proclamation of peace on earth
      anticipated the sight

Can your anxiety be worth
        scaring you into beating your ploughshares
      into swords?   No angel or demon
        can separate you   from the love of the Lord

THE ANGEL OF DEATH AT THE GRAND OLE OPRY

What do you know   O child of clay   of God & time?   I'm sent
to the bent   who'll soon ignite   like rags doused in turpentine
to unveil their worth before they alight

A boy cultivates sorrow in the bottle given   to ease his
                                                    stabbing spine
Despite his grave-bound trajectory   a music's arisen
so fine   it brings him to the Nashville Opry

    His every choice merges in disaster   lets it spill
        over those left to wait   lets it fill
            him with morphine & melancholy   lets it kill
                his marriage   & disparage his skill
                    so his voice verges on breaking

I'm not taking away his claim
to have seen the light   but when sorrow came
back in sight   he cut himself off   so lonesome he could die

When is time right for mercy   O child of clay?   I returned
what was left of Hank to Montgomery   Don't blame me
for cutting down the strong   Thank me for waiting so long

WHAT AN ANGEL ADMIRES

Is my fascination   with the subtle
dappling of a full forest   confusing
to you   or the way I still myself
on a pinnacle   where dawn radiates
across undulating desert?

You think your fields beneath me   in
more than a literal sense   or expect
the way your villages wrap around
the hillside   will be of no interest

You partner with the cliff edge   with
cypress   wall   & wisteria   building
from local stone   an admirable life
in harmony with all you've been given

Oh   if you saw how the eyeblue tinge
of your home   floats in space   you'd
feel its lyrical pull

-three-

The angels must often be astonished at us and think

we are the strangest creatures that well can be...

—CHARLES SPURGEON

AN ANGEL QUESTIONS OUR ANSWERS

We see you all love games   that show
how much you know   the puzzles
you're able to master   faster
than anyone   how you can piece
bits to fit   due to your expertise
But   please   descendant of dust
trust us   when we say   there's so much
more you don't get

Consider the birds   the flocks & herds
scattered   figuratively   on the hillside
Why would the good Lord
have chosen untamed words   for revealing
himself to you   scattered poetic analogies
concealing   what would have let
you settle comfortably into your knowing?
Why stories   a flash of sword

kaleidoscoping over flowing fields
forcing you from head   to heart?
Why such incarnations   half heard
on a steep slope   that vary with every telling
making you ponder   & wonder
& confess you only understand in part?
Please don't fight   about who's right
when together you share hope

JACOB WRESTLES

In the locust wind comes a rattle & hum...

Not one person had seen the encounter   for Jacob
         had sent them all across the Jabbok
toward his brother's sword   Now in the descending dark

on that stream's eastern shore   having long struggled with
         himself   he now faced the Angel of the Lord
As he braced himself for certain defeat
         only angels watched
& we wondered why it wasn't over in a heartbeat
         The animal-gasps of God
& man   told us what shadows tried to hide

The moon then rose on what's hard to describe
         the Fear in angelic
             yet physical
      form   locked in the grip of mere man
Jacob jabbed & grabbed   & daringly
         refused to let go
& received a kind wounding
         a fierce lesson in prayer

THE ANGELS WATCH YOU FALL

As angels we're not disinterested   Your
world has shrivelled   like a winter apple
to little more   than what you can see
a windfall   merely a physical thing
spiked with stubble   & slightly bruised
        Is denying what you've received
not forsaking those who've gone before?

As angels   we know you don't believe
though once   you followed trails
through fragile forests   to where cedars cling
to high cliffs   where the escarpment's edge
meets the sky   Yet   with your one fling
your purposes lost   in one moment   eternity
tossed off the ledge   with no knowledge
of who else would eventually pay

As angels we watch you fall   nothing
as dramatic as a leap from a bridge
or from a high ledge   but a fall
none-the-less
        Even we do not know   seeing your
severe descent from the lookout
if you might yet   lose faith
in your confident doubt

ANGEL DREAM

Once you lay your head on night's pillow
an angel may descend   Your dream   a conduit
for God's message   trickling unmistakably
into your upturned ear

When you stook your grain   why might
your brothers' sheaves bow to yours?   How now
could seven scrawny cows   eat seven much fatter ones?

It matters   O child of clay   who'd play
step-father to God's son   It matters which way
the stargazers took   on their way home

In these latter days   were we to beam
visions right into your night   might
you just dismiss them as a dream?

AN ANGEL SPEAKS OF EDEN'S FRUIT

If you suspect   a stranger might be angelic
whether shimmering or dim
I say   invite him in   & place fine food before him
Your poet   Milton   had Eden's Eve prepare
for one of the seraphim   a spread   she hoped might compare
since the same nourisher   formed the flavours for heaven's fare

Even now   to savour your fruit is worth
the descent to earth   but when she & Adam lived in obedience
        only the one tree left untried
Eden's fruit   would be a deeper delight
        quince & pears   growing there
        berries & cherries   mangoes & apricots
                unspoiled by rot   or pesticide

If you suspect   as you roll up the offramp   the strange man
waiting for passing change   in the cold & damp   might blow
any cash you give him   you might still roll down your window
        an apple held out in your hand

EAST OF EDEN

When first set at the east gate
we had to wait   & watch   & wonder
who might come by

Perched high   I let my eagle eye
roam to & fro across the earth   staring north to distant hills
& then beyond toward the pole

a cherub   among the cherubim   stationed toward
the rising sun from Eden   which brightly glistened on my
                                        mighty horns
the machinery of my sword revolving in its light

To the west   I turned my human form
& listened   where the storm of principalities & powers
glowered   as though they had control

Then   toward the south   a roar ripped
from my lion mouth   my fourth visage   guarding humanity
                                        from stumbling
into the dangers of the tree of life

But when steady waters flow through New Jerusalem
from the great giver's throne   the tree will grow   an orchard
                                        on both sides of the river
& you will be ready to taste & see   all that's good

AN ANGEL QUESTIONS OUR QUESTIONS

The one stone they repeatedly trip on
is order of operations   such as for clay
spun on the wet wheel of the universe
When was the formless void slapped down
as read of in verse two?   When   the start
& end of the first sunless day?

Did Adam find satisfaction   after the fall
working far from the garden?   Did God harden
Pharaoh's heart   against his will?   Were
the predestined   predestined   before
Yahweh considered who they'd be?
Were we   the angels   created before the purpose
given to us in creation?   When
did Lucifer choose not to obey?

The wisdom from Dante' s pen   *His eternity
outside of time*   still hasn't silenced such speculation

35

THIS SAME JESUS

So often you look at something
    without really seeing it   like when
        we saw you   & your ten friends
            staring into the sky

Later that day you couldn't say
    without first closing your eyes
        if the clouds had been   high
            & wispy or thick & glacier white

& we   not thinking of your shock
    at hopes yanked away then restored
        only saw the unblinking eyes
            of eleven men   turned toward heaven

though since your Lord   had just slipped
    from sight   your hearts burned
        & again might   whenever clouds come near
            to the way they appeared that day

ANGELIC MANIFESTATIONS

I could startle you awake   a surprise
in the night   or as an angel of light   I might trouble
your dream with my oration

I could go   where I'm bidden   hidden
in the guise of a man
        a strong-armed warrior   flowing hair
& flaming sword
        aglow as a shimmering youth
        or as a fabulous creature with multiple faces
wheels   lightning   horns   & wings   going
wherever the four winds blow

I could come in the clouds in a chariot
of fire   appearing according to his desire
attuned to the Triunity's
        call   & send
at a time   in a way   expected least
A single hand cannot applaud   but as an uninvited guest
at Belshazzar's feast   in mid-air   on his wall
I inscribed   the graffito of God
bringing a dynasty to its end

-four-

Millions of spiritual creatures
walk the earth unseen.

—HESIOD

THE ANGELS' VINEYARD SONG

Come sing with us a song   of our loved one's vineyard
        planted on a fertile hill   From heaven we watched him
till hard soil   clear weeds & stones   build wall   & well   & winepress
        Everything was done to ensure success   his loving selection
of choice vines   his skill in pruning & training them   along long wires
        to produce fine wines

But now   when he inquires after his due   the ungrateful children
        of his once faithful tenants   wonder who
he is   to ask anything of them   as though the vineyard just rose
        from the terrain   & *they've* made it grow
Oh how discomforted they will be   when he tears down its walls
        & commands the clouds   to hold back their rain

RAIN

Even angels love rain
        the way it
knows when to curl into haystack
clouds   & when to let go   spattering
leaves & grass   trickling along each
inner stem
        the way it
splatters dry dirt   & loudly clatters
like hooves   on tin roofs
        the way it
almost arrives   then blows by   high
on a dry wind that removes what
moisture remains   driving the prophet
to a raven-circled brook
        the way it
comes   when it comes   disrupting the dust
which puffs into the air   & then
drops in dampness   merging in mud
congealing together
        the way it
declares your dependence   little one
on the wind's whims   & divine design
        the way it
cuts ravines   & reminds you   how
your planet needs to be washed clean
& how   without watering   would
never grow anything

BIRDS OF THE AIR

Consider the birds of the air
how their ways on the wing   are so divergent
yet angel flight   you may be aware
isn't such a physical thing
We don't swing arm-like appendages
in urgent imitation of geese   rising from the river
with the vigor of an Olympian's butterfly
or Australian crawl   we don't fly in formation
& call   to one another of distant messages to deliver

Swallows scoop & snatch
      flies from the sky
      while they swoop & catch the air
      with aeronautic precision
eagles soar where mountains tower
vultures rely   on thermals
      to gloriously glide along a cliff edge
& hummingbirds gently lift
      above each flower

Only as physical as we choose to be   we are like
each of these   in flight   alternating
between weightlessness   & having the heft
to wield a fiery sword   unaffected
by windgusts & downpours   but you don't know
the turbulence of spiritual war we face   We whirl
& fight   like a First World War flying ace
like grackles assaulting a crow   bringing a word
from the Lord   across the sky with grace

FROZEN LAKE

The kingdom of heaven is like a child
skating out on a frozen lake   placing
a well-laced skate on a surface that would not
previously support her weight
like an angel stepping onto white cloud

Her shout   loud to racing friends
visibly rises in cold air   & helps her
soon forget   how her bare feet felt
just last summer   stepping down
into water along this same shore

The skater's blade   scrapes across the ice
wobbling a little at first   as she jabs
one skate   & then the other   into the hard
crystalline plane   gliding faster & faster
like a young bird in flight

Angels come & go   there are many things
we do not know   so perhaps
we'll watch her collapse
after her long hard skate   to see
what imprint she makes in the snow

POLAR BEAR

reflected in the eye of an angel

Are they not   the most angelic of beasts?   Bright
white   & mighty of limb   though hardly suited for flight
One thousand pounds of hypercarnivorous bear

O fragile child   what do you think   of the cub
seeing for the first time   their diminishing arctic icescape
stumbling after her mother from their winter lair?

Isolation has proven insufficient   the implications of wrong
radiate   to the ends of the earth   where
even inanimate ice crystals   wait

She knows nothing of changing seasons   or if all this drip
shrink   thaw   occurs for more ominous reasons
doesn't even know it hasn't been continuous   all winter long

Franklin dreamed of the Northwest Passage   in days before
supertankers   But do you dare allow it   knowing now
what such a trajectory could mean?

Does the mother bear notice   there's less sea ice?   Do you
O fragile child   on occasion   include the creation you're
to watch over   in your morning prayer?

YOUR CAT WATCHING

Let me set the quiet scene   Logs
crackled from the fireplace   as you
gathered around the dinner table

Perhaps you'd just said grace   & as
you reached for serving bowls   your
peace was pierced by your cat's

howling screech   Unable to perceive
what had changed   you all turned   to
where the cat sat strangely watching

empty air
            You all turned to face   *us*
angels   whose intent had simply been

to observe without being observed
equally startled by that caterwaul   &
then the curious stare   of your whole

family   before someone shrugged
There's nothing there   Your cat's eyes
burned   with a narrowing glare   that

seemed might yet give us away   so I
turned her way   & she went yowling
up the stairs

CORAM DEO

Matthew 18:10

I know what is to you unknown   little one
From my place before the throne   I alone
observe the fleshy flexing of your heart
its leap as you pursue your treasure
& how each of your tiny faith gestures
brings the Master pleasure

I was first flown   like a bolt of lightning
from God's glance   like a wind   blown
across the galaxies   to watch life's spark
suture soul to body   according to no
previously existing pattern
in your mother's womb

You lie prone in your helplessness   little one
unsure as to whether your groans are heard
not expecting to be nurtured   yet you are   & then
before you know it   you're grown   Even I have not been
                                                    shown
your secret name   the one to be engraved on white stone
or know his good plans for your future

AN ANGEL FROM SIGNORELLI'S *RESURRECTION OF THE BODY*

San Brizio Chapel, Orvieto

I blow my trumpet   earth-shakingly loud
I & one other   standing on cloud
with banners unfurled   marking
this moment   the world's waited for
through all of creation's groans

The bones rattle   unscatter   recompose
Some skeletons chose   not to wait to be re-fleshed
Surprisingly refreshed   each skull arose
to the delight of being undead   First just the heads
push from soil   like lilies' spring surging   & those

in fresh flesh   unrotting   unbroken   unworn
uninterned   disdiseased   not even sick
as every clock refuses to tick
they pull themselves up   like swimmers emerging
on a summer dock

Those merely bones   take on flesh
The fleshed   take on clothes
They gather to converse   to embrace those
they'd lost   to dance & praise
finding in our trumpet call   the Father's music

AN ANGEL FROM CIMABUE'S
THE CRUCIFIXION

Basilica Di San Francesco, Assisi

We fill the sky as we fly

The visible & invisible glow from the fresco
where grimacing Pharisees   under their breath
discuss what will soon be completed

How could they know   of the coming reversal
when noon's drowned in night   black
overtakes white   before death is forever defeated?

Circling the Saviour   we're the angels they don't see
as Cimabue must have done   His pigments once showed
our true colours   before time left them depleted

He imagined Francis bowing   before God's son
a sublime behaviour   that   by everyone
one day will be repeated

-five-

Every visible thing in this world
is put in the charge of an angel.

—AUGUSTINE

SITTING ON A STONE

Angels expect to happen   what we've been told
will happen   unlike you   or that old man
overawed by incense   & Gabriel's presence
who stammered
     How can this be done?
when told in their old age
he & his wife would have a son   Why
shouldn't the archangel strike him dumb?

Herod was worse   hammered against
what Micah foretold   brought his shocking
sceptre   down on every baby's head
     & then   even the fishermen
questioned among themselves
what they'd been clearly shown

So try not to hold   my mocking tone
against me when I said   *Why
do you seek the living among the dead?*
as I sat on that rolled-away stone

INTERVENING ANGEL

To Moriah I flew   ready to wing
to Abraham's aid   while his servants
remained with the donkey   & he laid
wood   on the youth's shoulder
but I was detained

I thought I could help   when Abraham
did not falter   built the altar
from large boulders   & laid
out the wood
but I was held back

I was not slack in crossing the skies
when Abraham bound Isaac
but I was prevented   I now realize
so he might head straight
for the brink

That's when he raised the knife
& I think he then knew   that he loved God
more than God's promises   more than
God' s blessing   even more
than his son   & his own life

That's when I was able to tell
my message   seizing
the old man's wrist
& that's when the knife fell

LIBERATING ANGEL

I won't explain how molecules
merely need to be pushed aside
        why shackles   on stone   won't
clatter when they fall
        how iron doors silently swing
open on their own

        You seem troubled by things
that do not trouble me
        those two chains   or the
guards they're tethered to
        the still soldiers who will not
waken as we pass

        Shuffling your feet   you haven't
caught on   this is not a dream
        We walk   out into the street
into the darkness of night
        I look in your face   one last time
& vanish from your sight

AVENGING ANGEL

So you thought no one would notice
as you wrung another nickel out of the naïve pensioner

who misplaced her trust in you
From what she ventured   you gained

slipping in another service charge for services
not rendered   defence not given   compassion feigned

amusing yourself   for profit
at her expense   taking what she couldn't give

& live   making her turn down the heat
to meet monthly payments   from her narrow

income   forcing her to the soup kitchen down the street
Have you forgotten   what prophets proclaimed   not known

my flaming sword would separate bone from marrow
& that whatever does not balance   will be found wanting?

Where now is your Mercedes to comfort you   that heap
of crushed metal on the highwayside?   With mercy withheld

all you've ever loved lies smouldering   your nostrils fill
with the burning stench of your own miserable hide

MINISTERING ANGEL

A dusty track curves into the wilderness   Two walk
eventually veering from that road   across a land of dry stones
one in physical form led by one unseen

We hover   just beyond his perception
waiting & watching as he's left to walk
deeper into desert   alone   on his slow
slow fast   At his lowest point of bodily
ability   he's offered devilbread   an all-
for-nothing chance   a birth-right deal
a piece of fruit dangling from a forbidden
branch   He's offered a glorious Kidron
Valley swandive into fame   & a means-
justifying   short-cut to a name
above every name

It is written   he replies
& as Satan skulks away   we bring better bread
& rest from all those lies

A GUARDIAN ANGEL
IN THE DOMINICAN REPUBLIC

Asked to keep our charges safe
our task   is so much harder here
with so many more stones to strike
their feet against   blood pressure
heat   bug bites   water-borne parasites
& faster deaths to fear   through
bad booze   or natural disaster   such as
hurricane   & flood
& daily motorized risks
for helmetless riders   switching lanes
a swarm of buzzing motorbikes   swung
back & forth   like stitching needles
a father & mother   with treasure in her arms
& boss-deciders' half-measures
for safety   not wanting to spend any more
& limited medical help
within reach for the poor
Asked to keep our charges safe
our task   is so much harder here

A GATHERING ANGEL TRIES
TO STAY ALERT

As fig twigs turn tender   & leaves start to unfold
summer is soon   We've been told   similarly

to be ready for the sender to say   *It's time*
but let's not pretend   wars & rumours of wars

on earth are rare   How can that make us
any more aware?   Wherever vultures circle

there's a carcass below   in the valley of the shadow
or high in the hills   Two baristas grinding with their mills

one is right-handed   the other left   all the people
eating & drinking   getting ready for the wedding season

Though not allowed to know   I must still be ready
for when the King of glory comes in the clouds

IN THE EARLY MORNING

angel dance

In the early morning   with the dew   do you
ever wander through   a grassy meadow
& wonder   at the joyous presence?
        Not the redwinged blackbird
who has already flown down to the pond
        Not the dragonflies hovering
above the sun-warmed path   Something stirs the glade
& seems like a childhood dream
We come to watch the likes of you   little one
overflowing with the joy of what's been made

In the early morning   in your country
when we descend   there's little for you to see
unless   like Emily   as each angel passes
through green leaves & brown grasses   you notice them bend
        We come in search of a place
a church-like field   swaying with Queen Anne's lace
where a breeze is enough to make
the shimmering shasta daisies dance
which they may   with or without a wisp of wind

In the early morning   angels are drawn
to the celebration of the hillside   & at times inhabit the wild
So come   dance with us   child

AN ANGEL WATCHES *IT'S A WONDERFUL LIFE*

Angels   when talking   aren't like stars
blinking with a loose connection
We don't show each other
such human condescension
& aren't like pilots-in-training
needing to earn our wings

When Clarence first appears
who can see him as an angel?
Does his presence   bring fear
his luminescence   make anyone quiver?
No one needs a reassuring   *fear not*
even when the whirlwind
almost knocks the door off
above the swirling river

When his pockets are empty
George Bailey senses some error
rather than angelic terror
If our Commander were to deliver
an angel appearing as Clarence
that's not what would really be there
& yet   the thing that rings true
is this intervention's due   to Zuzu' s prayer

-*six*-

Walk carefully, in all thy ways, as one with whom
the angels are present as he has given them charge.

—BERNARD OF CLAIRVAUX

THE ANGEL OF THE CHURCH IN TORONTO WRITES

So many lamps have gone out   but the fragrance
    from many others   rises to heaven
seven times seven   times seven   times seven

    times seven   Like other angels
I have been redeployed   given
    a new lampstand to tend

to strengthen the few who'll remain to the end
    those in clothes of white   with ears to hear
& so I write   Once known as Toronto the Good

    every neighbourhood interspersed with spires
your city stood   for what it thought was right
    Now   overshadowed by condo blocks

you're distracted by worldly cares
    Now   you dwell in a spiritual structure
resembling Van Gogh's Church at Auvers

    Do you know the difference between
your poverty   & that which makes you rich   between
    the narrow way   where you once walked

& the briar-tangled ditch   between ice & fire
    in the parch-throated choir   & the terrible
apathetic middle   where so many celebrate

    what they   should never tolerate?
I call on you to recall   the height
    from which you've fallen

THE BURNING HEART

an angel addresses a king

You carefully construct your heart   surround
it with aqueducts   & gardens   place it in gold
casing concealing its flame

raise high your name   raise your image higher
lifting up   lifting up   never burning down
except those distant   resistant

cities & towns   & now these few who refuse
the slight due   you require   Your dire
arsonist heart doesn't differentiate

melts white-hot metal   burns wood   scorches skin
Exponentially higher   you turn up the heat
to have three defiers   cast in

Nothing can survive your blast   & yet you see
a fourth figure has joined   the other three
an angel   walking with them   in the heart of the fire

AN ANGEL ON MARRIED LOVE

Not everything is to be done   on earth
as it is in heaven   As the angelic host
the earthly unknown   that puzzles us most
is   the first   *not good*   was about man being alone
　　We don't understand   all we hear & see
of a man's life   While at work   when he pauses
to think on his dear wife   it causes
him to smile
　　When Eve first walked the garden
as graceful as a young gazelle   we saw her
as God's finest creation   but even before she
shared the fruit   Adam was under her spell
　　We're not saying her voice
overpowered his choice   he knew
they were disobeying   So when they fell
was his error   rather than in placing her above himself
　　　　for we've heard even earthly love   *always*
　　　　trusts   always hopes   is not self-seeking
nor even in desiring what that taste could bring
but far greater   in placing her   above their creator?

67

CHERUBIM

Our wings are quartets of glory   & our fourfold faces turn
toward the round earth's imagined corners   giving you
    a framework   O child of clay   against which to view
new experience   But when you hear
    your prophet's murky descriptions
you struggle to sense   whether they're symbolic
    or physically real   fitting the way things appear

To cope   with images of wheels within wheels   is it worth
picturing pulleys   cogs   reels   or a gyroscope?   Your mind
is seeing   machine-like beings   turning & burning
somehow horned   & covered with eyes   a disguise where faces
    are formed   somewhat like certain creatures of earth

When tree branches wave   as frantically as women
whose children are being carried away
    you call it   *wind*   When blinding beams stream
from behind a stormcloud   you acknowledge   *light*
    But how could a prophet make such disorientation clear?
When you see us   whirring & conferring
    picking glowing coals   bare-handed   from the fire
do not fear   The familiar conceals
    as much as it reveals

SERAPHIM

The thresholds & the doorposts shook
as praises to the king were sung
I see now in your downcast look
your burdens birthed in every flaw
your smudging fingers   tainted tongue
& grief because of what you saw
We hide our faces with our wings
then cover feet with one more pair
& *holy   holy   holy* sing
while with a third stay in the air

AN ANGEL ADDRESSES A CHURCHGOER

I   Painting

You stand before what Rembrandt shared
little one   perplexed   & then perturbed
for the figures   flanking the father
should not be there

I know you know   this can be no literal rendering
for the parabolic father ran to where
he saw his son   *a long way off*   so this scene
would not have been   played out in their presence

II   Poem

You puzzle over the page   where the poet's poem plays
but won't stay put   jumping from parable to parable
& then ricocheting off   to the far reaches of the universe
without ever telling us what it means

III   Parable

You resent feeling uncertain   as the father
scans the horizon   *How can this patriarch represent*
God   unsure when his son's returning   turning
eyes from bad behaviour   showing favour

to the younger   despite the elder son's track record?
You reach for your stack of commentaries
their momentary relief from mystery   their promised link
to what   & how   to think

AN ANGEL'S ASKED ABOUT WILLIAM BLAKE

You ask   Was the young William Blake truthful
saying he saw a tree filled with angels   their wings
glistening on every bough   or was he sailing
dangerously close   to the shipwreck of a beating
weighing how far   he dare frame such a fearful fallacy?
     You say   Perhaps they were just birds
& young William was playing with words
     Such an incident   if it ever occurred
would be less memorable to the heavenly host
most would hardly notice   a scruffy kid
on a London street   even looking up into their tree
     Was he visionary   his eyes bugging wide
in an apprenticeship of perceiving   having seen
what others could not see   or did he express his believing
as though it were visible   stretching the faith he sought?
     You ask   Was he mad   not knowing what was real
or was he   trying to test his perceptions?
     I say   Good questions

AN ANGEL DENIES A FLAT EARTH

If it were my place   O descendent of dust   I would
help you face facts   the world's not flat
    beyond your horizon   the ocean
curves   like where the smooth skin on a child's shoulder
curves   down onto her back
    you could circumnavigate
the globe without falling off
    though your world may feel flat
enrichment awaits
    & things your senses cannot sense
still make sense   creation opening its mouth
wider than a hippopotamus could
    like that closet door you've never opened
at the back of the storeroom   which is not
a closet door at all   but a way out
of your wearying workplace   which leads to the back lot
& above that   to the treetops   & above that
to the stars   & above that   beyond the beyond
where there's far more than you've ever dreamed

AN ANGEL SPEAKS OF LIVING THINGS

There's the high   & there's the low
like sky to dirt   O child of clay
yet no angel would ever show
distain for such as you
For unlike the manta ray or bat
the rat   or blue jay
      all true in design
you   though tumbled   sullied
      toxified   & crushed flat
you were modelled after the divine

There's the high   & there's the low
like eagle to earthworm   though
human worth is higher   Even those
whose minds have bent their bodies
whose bodies have stained their souls
still glow   like sacred fire
      All angels know the shock
though lost on you   when celestial will
left the highest place   & took on your form
      to be made low

-seven-

...the joy of the angels lies only in obedience
to God's will...

—JOHN NEWTON

THE TENTH PLAGUE

the angel of death waits

For your reputation's sake   you've stiffened
from the inside out   not impressed   by tricks
with snakes & sticks   rigid poles wriggling
across cold tile   only to be swallowed whole
    I am the angel who waits

A slave cries out   at a surging crimson wave
while dawn shimmers on the Nile
Your crocodilian heart   refuses to fear
this red blood   as dead stench floods the air
as if all is governed by the likes of Sobek & Ra
& you're part of their pantheon

But once it's gone   rising from the river
a coarse croaking comes   fat-bellied frogs
hopping across your floor   with no regard
for your station   in a thrumming invasion
that slaps & plops   beyond all control
until their predetermined dying   has them raked
into heaps that reek of broken promises
    while I await my call

Then next small specks   lift from the dust
in a hex your gods can't replicate   to creep
on your skin & in your bed   Akratic
you scritch & scratch at crawling creatures
    while I wait
Then swarms descend   flies   with the bulging eyes
of your imagined deity   buzzing about your head
your cattle are struck dead   & all you've said are lies
    so still I wait

It's like some hell   you drag the land through
before the death angel is summoned
                    & so I come
a juggernaut of fear   an unstoppable flood
looking for where there's no smeared blood
a dark shadow   falling on the window
a silent step on the stair   a child's last breath
on his pillow   a mother crying   in both palace
& hovel   for what's no longer there
All this   Pharaoh   for your reputation's sake

MURDER MYSTERY

an angel puzzles over Dorothy Sayers

Why the interest in crime   such a skilled
writer investigating that curse?   From an angelic
perspective   at first   it seemed worse
than a waste of time   her focus filled
with grievous acts   Never mind   the facts

being fictitious   a nonexistent victim killed
by an imagined killer   the body dumped
in a stranger's bath   I wondered   What's got
into her?   What about thinking on the honest
the just   the pure?

Why stare so intently into darkness   until shadows
take shape & grow particular?   Any angel can tell you
it all comes from sin   A young wife & her lover   hide
their affair   in her mind   she's justified   Later
when her husband's lost his life   does it matter

murder or suicide?   To trace injury back to jealousy
or how an indiscretion may lead
to a lie   & a lie to violence for the sake of silence
only shows the human heart   So   Dorothy
I'm beginning to see   how what you do

is a way of getting at the true   stumping
readers   who'll catch themselves   jumping
to false conclusions   & hinting at a greater mystery
how justice will one day come through
though for now   only the angels see

TEEN ANGEL

an angel gets annoyed by a pop song

What is it about your little girlfriend
O child of clay   that makes you sing of her as an angel?
Is she a terrible being of fire & light
able to mete out destruction & death?

Does God's judgement linger on her breath?
Her foresight seems far from prophetic
her insight pathetic   rushing back to the car   broken
on the tracks   for some sentimental token

It fits for a hit record   but in a limited way
for when eighty-one hundred tons of rushing steel
steals her earthly future   why wouldn't that fling away
the ring clutched in her fingers?

I'm weary of the worn out *up above*   rhyming
with *love*   & dead dolts in cartoons sprouting wings
Death does not make you higher beings
That's not how it loses its sting

AN ANGEL EXPAINS PRAYER

You make the simple so complicated   little one
but then to explain   I may need to make it more complicated
still   It involves the Master's triunity   how Number Three
translates   & Number Two advocates   though Number One
knows what's going on before one word is said
   It's like when you whisper   *Dear God*   I carry
your intentions to the skies   although it's not me carrying
them at all   One million angels circle the Master   besides
the six-winged seraphim who are always singing praise   each
has their prayer-burdens to share   but when I arrive   it's like
a tornado that can't touch me   all's a blur in the whirl of wings
& wonder   there's a hum of voices & trumpets   & then
his eyes lock on mine   & nothing else is there but your prayer
& his compassionate stare
   Simply put   you speak   & without interrupting
a single raindrop in mid fall   the universe
& everything beyond the universe   more than stops
has stopped   ceases   in anticipation of ceasing
& the magnitude of magnitude   the magnificence of
magnificence bends
enthralled with your turning in his direction
with the very sigh of your being   drawn heavenward
   Prayer too   little one   is when he reaches out to you
but by that point you've usually lost focus
distracted by   his apparent silence
your prayer's eloquence   or   perhaps
the fine design of your shoes

PREANNUNCIATION

She seems like a shadow   no
luminosity to her   a village girl in the
        village gloom

What might she say as I enter the
room   bringing a brightness   beyond
        her ken?

I scan the street   until I've caught her
wait   & watch   as she returns with water
        from the town's only well

I don't want to astound her   make
her flee in fear   or confound her with
        the things she'll hear

How will she receive my greeting   as I
tell   she's highly favoured   how will
        I enable her to see?

Might she think she's unsavoury   too
lowly   too young   or simply submit
        & say   *Let it be*?

SKY CHOIR

Were you to see a light-pierced night   & hear
our sky choir   voices echoing cloud to ground
our message   though it comes through loud & clear
might still be lost in overwhelming sound
Our angel glory   like a pale moon
just sings of greater light   so you may know
our lyrics flung   & sung   of now & soon
our   *Gloria in excelsis Deo*
You may   O child of clay   at first be drawn
as if our spectacle might be what matters
but like a summer bloom it will be gone
& like the winter ice it soon will shatter
So turn away from angel wing & feather
& join us as we praise his name forever

SWING LOW SWEET GROCERY CART

an angel transposes II Kings 2 into the 21st century

When Elijah & Elisha
crossed all eight lanes of the hectic 410
every Toyota & tractor-trailer   in full trajectory
along the highway   was flash frozen
as in a still photograph   after Elijah'd struck
the pavement with his rolled-up jacket

When the roar of traffic
resumed behind them   Elisha turned & saw fifty men
on the opposite slope   like parents
faithfully watching a playoff game

Suddenly a whirlwind of flame
like the cartoon Tasmanian devil   came
between them   like a shimmering grocery cart
pulled by heavenly horses   Elisha let out a cry
& Elijah was taken up   more swiftly
than fighter jets can fly

Then Elisha struck the pavement   & once again
crossed all eight lanes of the busy 410
receiving the fifty prophets' esteem
though they didn't quite get   what they'd just seen

RESPONSE TO RILKE

There are few angels   to firsthand hear your cries
         for some circle the earth
                  turning away terrors you've no knowledge of
                  struggling against principalities
who try to taint   whatever seems worthwhile
         while the seraphim who dwell above
bring perpetual praise
                  sing sonnets before the face of God
who exists always   before every living thing
in that space   where flowers endlessly open
         & others have been commissioned to care
for the redeemed   for churches   for children   for saints

& though I once was called   to oversee your sojourn
it was never mine   to turn you left or right
                  or hold you in my embrace
You have no angel   it's true   to turn to in your need
no human   no animal   & obviously no tree
but don't think   that leaves you
with no source of consolation
We are merely messengers   & would direct you
         with a passion that would consume us like flame
to burn   & be burned   for the glory of the name
to be an ash   that rises   & then falls

SURREAL ORCHID

an angel speaks of faith

Picture an orchid   one you can physically feel   planted
        in your very physical body
Roots reach through your liver   kidneys   spleen
        stabilize their organic soil
Leaves   though hidden   spread their curving green
        while the stem & branches
branch & bloom into your heart & lungs
        fill your every breath
with holy fragrance   your heartbeat with resonance
        As buds form on branch tips
& buds turn to blossoms   the blossoms
        though unseen   make life gleam

This is not to say   some haven't suffered dormant seasons
        when the inner orchid seems
like a dried-out stick   For some this drives them to despair
        to deny the orchid's even there
to kick hope aside   & suppress its eventual renewal
        with a gloved hand
shoving the dream of tendrils down   or ripping any trace
        from their own throats

Did you know   dear child   nurturing this orchid's
        your most crucial task?
Let it encircle your heart   let it fill your brain
        with its delicate fulgour
let it be the fulfillment to the prayer
        you most frequently ask

Acknowledgements

Thanks to the editors of the following publications, where many of these poems first appeared:

Alliance Connection—"This Same Jesus"

Amethyst Review—"Angelic Manifestations," "In the Early Morning"

ARTS—"An Angel's View of Automobiles"

Christian Century—"An Angel Laughs about Laundry," "Staircase," "An Angel Critiques Caravaggio's *Saint Matthew & the Angel*," "Polar Bear," "Sitting on a Stone"

Christian Courier—"Learning to Fly"

Dappled Things—"An Angel Marvels at Human Language"

Ekstasis—"An Angel's Asked about William Blake"

Event—"What an Angel Admires," "The Burning Heart"

Faith Today—"An Angel from Cimabue's *The Crucifixion*"

Leaf—"Fear Not," "Reflection for Elizabeth Barrett Browning," "The Angels' Vineyard Song," "Birds of the Air," "A Guardian Angel in the Dominican Republic"

The Other Journal—"The Angel of Death at the Grand Ole Opry"

Pensive—"Rain"

Practical Theology—"Of Angels Speaking," "Curiously More," "Angel Dream," "East of Eden," "The Tenth Plague." "This work was first published in *Practical Theology* 'D.S. Martin (2020) Five Angel Poems, Practical Theology, 13:3, 306-308, DOI: 10.1080/1756073X.2020.1748334'"

Relief—"Angel of Revolution," "Response to Rilke"

The Society—"Your Cat Watching"

Solum Literary Journal—"An Angel Questions Our Answers," "Seraphim,"
"Cherubim"

St. Austin Review—"An Angel Questions Our Questions," "The Angels Watch
You Fall," "An Angel from Signorelli's *Resurrection
of the Body*," "Surreal Orchid"

Whale Road Review—"Swing Low Sweet Grocery Cart"

The Windhover—"Ministering Angel," "An Angel Explains Prayer"

The poem "Ministering Angel" was also reprinted in *Alliance Connection*.

Although a writer's task is by nature solitary, I have found my work en-
riched and encouraged by dozens of people I'd like to thank. I'll trim the
list this time around to: Jill Peláez Baumgaertner, Mark S. Burrows, Brad
Davis, John F. Deane, John & Marion Franklin (Imago), Malcolm Guite,
Nathaniel Lee Hansen, Dave Hearn, Burl Horniachek, Andrew Lansdown,
Sydney Lea, Stan & Wendy Porter (McMaster Divinity College), Joe Ricke,
Luci Shaw, Gerard Smyth, James Tughan, John Van Rys, and Ralph Wood.
I am honoured by those poets who have permitted me to speak into their
art. Thanks also to the family of my heart, the friends of my writers group,
and our dear friends (Iain & Margaret) who have weathered the pandemic
with us.

The Poiema Poetry Series

COLLECTIONS IN THIS SERIES INCLUDE:

Six Sundays toward a Seventh by Sydney Lea
Epitaphs for the Journey by Paul Mariani
Within This Tree of Bones by Robert Siegel
Particular Scandals by Julie L. Moore
Gold by Barbara Crooker
A Word In My Mouth by Robert Cording
Say This Prayer into the Past by Paul Willis
Scape by Luci Shaw
Conspiracy of Light by D.S. Martin
Second Sky by Tania Runyan
Remembering Jesus by John Leax
What Cannot Be Fixed by Jill Pelaez Baumgaertner
Still Working It Out by Brad Davis
The Hatching of the Heart by Margo Swiss
Collage of Seoul by Jae Newman
Twisted Shapes of Light by William Jolliff
These Intricacies by David Harrity
Where the Sky Opens by Laurie Klein
True, False, None of the Above by Marjorie Maddox
The Turning Aside anthology edited by D.S. Martin
Falter by Marjorie Stelmach
Phases by Mischa Willett
Second Bloom by Anya Krugovoy Silver
Adam, Eve, & the Riders of the Apocalypse anthology edited by D.S. Martin
Your Twenty-First Century Prayer Life by Nathaniel Lee Hansen
Habitation of Wonder by Abigail Carroll
Ampersand by D.S. Martin
Full Worm Moon by Julie L. Moore
Ash & Embers by James A. Zoller
The Book of Kells by Barbara Crooker
Reaching Forever by Philip C. Kolin
The Book of Bearings by Diane Glancy
In a Strange Land anthology edited by D.S. Martin
What I Have I Offer With Two Hands by Jacob Stratman
Slender Warble by Susan Cowger
Madonna, Complex by Jen Stewart Fueston
No Reason by Jack Stewart
Abundance by Andrew Lansdown

www.ingramcontent.com/pod-product-compliance
Lightning Source LLC
LaVergne TN
LVHW041201080426
835511LV00006B/695